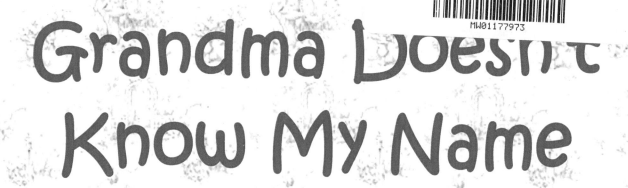

Grandma Doesn't Know My Name

Written by Joy Shepherd

Illustrated by Karalee Hammes

Other books by Joy Shepherd
   The Monster in My Room
Please visit Joyshepherd.com to see more about the author.

Other books Illustrated by Karalee Hammes
   Leonard the Lion Loves Salad
   The Monster in My Room
Please see more about the illustrator at graphicalreflections.com

Grandma Doesn't Know My Name

Copyright 2016

Published June 16, 2017

ISBN-13: 978-1544144122
ISBN-10: 1544144121

DEDICATION
With love to mom and dad, who taught me all about thankfulness..

It is my wish that *Grandma Doesn't Know My Name* will assist families in acknowledging the love that continues despite the challenges of Alzheimer's. Dr. Black, I am grateful for your dedication and commitment in finding a cure.

NOTE TO PARENTS

Dr. Sandra E. Black, O.C., O.Ont., MD, FRCP(C), FRSC, FAAN, FAHA, FANA
Alzheimer's and other dementias affect 48 million people worldwide, over 9 million in North America alone with the numbers expected to double by 2030.
Grandma Doesn't Know My Name does a wonderful job helping children learn to accept these changes, even if they can't understand them. The story puts a light-hearted spin on the confusion and sometimes hurt that can occur when a grandparent cannot recall a beloved grandchild's name. This heartwarming story focuses on what matters most –
the love that endures and the positive playful interactions that are still alive, despite the hurdles that come with Alzheimer's.
This story is an excellent read for children, parents, teachers, caregivers and loved ones.

Dr. Sandra Black holds the Brill Chair in Neurology, Department of Medicine, Sunnybrook Health Sciences Center and University of Toronto
Hurvitz Brain Sciences Research Program Director, Sunnybrook Research Institute
Executive Director, Toronto Dementia Research Alliance, U of Toronto

iPad is a trademark of Apple Inc.

Joy Shepherd

My name is the same,
it hasn't changed,

But grandma doesn't know my name.

She can hear when I sing and see this is me,

and watch as I climb and
sit on her knee.

But everything is not the same,

cuz grandma doesn't know my name.

Grandma does not have any pain,
her memory isn't
working in her brain.

Lots and
lots of things
have
changed,

like doing
puzzles and
playing games.

Grandma think of the fun things
we will do,

When my mom brings me to
spend time with you .

I'll bring my iPad and download
some songs,

and write down words so you can sing along.

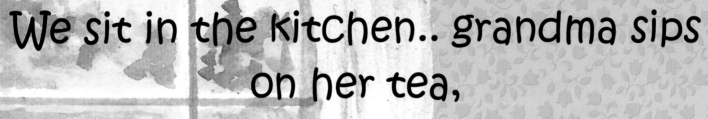

We sit in the kitchen.. grandma sips
on her tea,

We color with crayons
just grandma and me .

I start to draw ..grandma by my side,

I color a picture of
how I feel inside.

When I show it to her,
she has tears in her eyes.

You are the colors of the rainbow
that shine so bright
You are my sun in the morning
and my moon at night

XXOOX

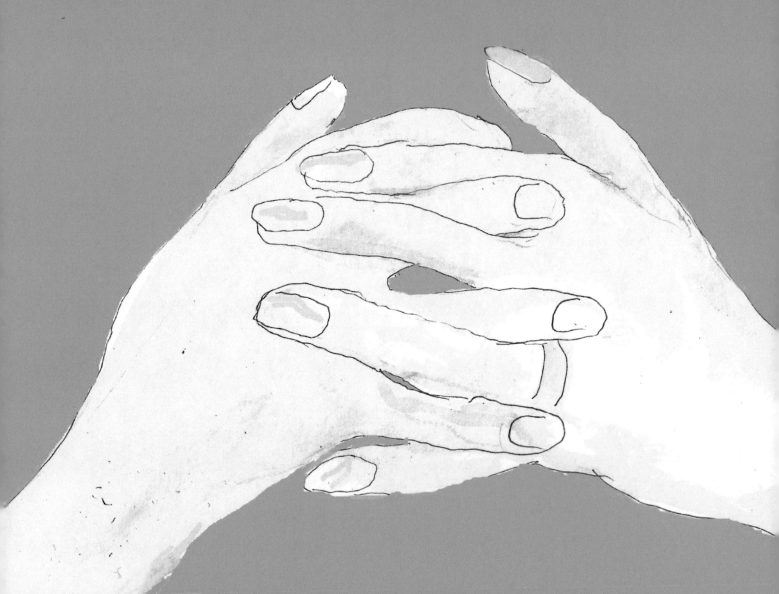

I take her hands..
and hold them high
"I love you grandma
bigger than the sky"

She hugs me tight..
it feels the same
as she looks at the picture..
and reads my name.

ACKNOWLEDGMENTS

Sue-Ellen Welfonder;
Thank you for inspiring me to bring pen to paper.

Dr. Sandra E. Black, O.C., O.Ont., MD, FRCP(C), FRSC
Thank You for your wisdom and assistance in the
development of this story. I would like to acknowledge your
caring and compassion for patients and families impacted
by Alzheimer's disease.

Dr. Roz Doctorow, EdD (Dr. of Education)
Thank you for your friendship and invaluable editorial
advice in bringing this book to life.

Karalee Hammes, Illustrator
 Thank you for your wonderful talents, hours of
patience...always with a smile.

Write and Draw
Your Feelings!

Made in the USA
Columbia, SC
30 June 2017